DANGEROUS
GOD

DANGEROUS GOD

WRATH, VENGEANCE, RECOMPENSE, AND TERROR

STUDY GUIDE

Jim Albright

As you cannot judge a book by its cover, so in this case you cannot judge a book by its title. *Dangerous God* is actually a book of good news—terrifyingly good news—because it is a book full of truth about God. Admittedly, it is truth about God that is often overlooked, ignored, or even denied, but it is truth, nonetheless. It is also hard truth in the sense that instead of giving us "warm fuzzies," it causes cold shivers. But it is good truth in that it corrects the lopsided view of God that is common in contemporary Christianity. If you want to know God more as He reveals Himself in the Bible than as we think we want Him to be, you'll be grateful for this book.

DONALD S. WHITNEY: Professor of Biblical Spirituality and Associate Dean, The Southern Baptist Theological Seminary, Louisville, Kentucky; USA

Jim Albright balances our typically skewed view of God by showing us that he is not only merciful, but also wrathful. Euphemistic thinking about God is not truthful thinking about God. God, in fact, is more merciful than we have ever thought because His just judgment is more severe than we have ever thought. This book, as shocking as it might be, is a needed corrective.

JIM ELLIFF: President of Christian Communicators Worldwide and a founding pastor of Christ Fellowship of Kansas City, Missouri, USA

Jim Albright's latest book is an excellent summary of the often-forgotten doctrines of God's wrath and judgment. He calls believers to a serious reconsideration of our weak contemporary ideas of God as merely loving. This book provides a sobering call to the biblical reality of the wrath of God and an honest reminder of the consequences of ignoring the God who judges all.

JIM EHRHARD: Ph.D. of Theology, Professor at Kiev Theological Seminary, Kiev, Ukraine

Christianity in America has become very man-centered, resulting in the avoidance and neglect of God's wrath, vengeance, recompense, and terror. When I think deeply about a being who will condemn human souls to an eternity of torment but also gladly sacrificed His only Son to a gruesome death to save human souls in rebellion against Him, I'm left in wonderment. Albright focuses on the attributes of God we naturally avoid but so desperately need if we are truly seeking the one, true, living God. As I read *Dangerous God*, the Lord's Spirit deflated my pride, exposed my man-centeredness, and rekindled my fear of the Lord to the praise of His glory and the joy of my soul.

BRAD VADEN: Pastor of Grace Baptist Church, Scott, Arkansas, USA

Albright's new book, *Dangerous God*, is not like any other book you will likely find in the twenty-first century. Albright dares to declare the true nature of the God who inhabits the universe. Many pastors and authors in our fearful-of-offending-others culture shy away from speaking about the true God of the Bible—a God of wrath, anger, and vengeance against sin and sinners. . .but Jim's book doesn't contain a single "shy" word in it. Jim's not interested in presenting a huggable God that the modern church can easily relate to, but the majestic God that is, the God in whose presence man should tremble. And he's convinced that getting to know this God, and not the domesticated God you've most likely been presented, is the best thing that can happen to you. To live a life in the fear and awe of the living God is truly to live a life worth living.
KEITH JONES: Missionary and Founding Pastor of Centro Veritas Church, Milan, Italy

We are quick to use the word "saved" when we refer to people coming to faith in Jesus. We often say, "We are saved from our sins." To somehow believe that we have been saved from something to do with us is a grave error. When through faith in Christ we are saved, we are saved from the wrath of Almighty God. Jim's book shows just what we are saved from and, on the flipside, what we are facing if we do not accept Jesus. This is a no-holds-barred exposé of the God no one wants to talk about because we have applied a "political correctness" filter to our twenty-first-century god that makes Him easier to accept. This book is written in love. It is one of the most honest books about the One True God. You owe it to yourself, your loved ones, and your neighbors to read it.
ALAN JOHNSTON: Ordained Minister in the Presbyterian Church of Ireland since 1998; Pastor of Killinchy Presbyterian Church

Dangerous God: STUDY GUIDE
Wrath, Vengeance, Recompense, and Terror
Copyright © 2022 by Jim Albright

ISBN: 978-1-7359491-9-2

This guide is intended for use with the author's earlier book,
Dangerous God: Wrath, Vengeance, Recompense, and Terror
ISBN: 978-1-7343452-7-8

www.dangerousgod.com

Cover design and typeset by www.greatwriting.org
Cover design consultation: Jim Albright / Jim Holmes

Great Writing Publications
Taylors, SC
www.greatwriting.org

PREFACE

At Dangerous God Ministries, we are posing what we believe to be the most important question before the professing Christian. Are you worshiping the one true God? The biblical God? The God who is? The God who, in Scripture, repeatedly reveals His wrath, vengeance, recompense, and terror in judgment?

God is both unrepentant and unapologetic regarding His awful majesty and fearsome greatness. He has unashamedly revealed exactly who He is for every intelligent being to behold and consider. Certainly, it is long past time for His church to simply open the Book and behold all that He has made known about Himself. It is time for His people to tremble afresh and anew!

This study guide is intended to be used in a thirteen-session group study that focuses on the book *Dangerous God*. It is designed to not only help cover the biblical material but to also challenge the participants to examine their own notions about God. . .namely, whether they are biblical or not.

Our prayer is that God would use the book *Dangerous God* and this study guide to awaken a consuming desire within the Christian to know all the disclosed fullness of Yahweh—for to look at the unedited God of the Bible is to never be the same. And as Albright asks, "Aren't you way past ready to go on with God? Aren't you ready for Him to blow up your heart, soul, and mind yet again?"

Please consider joining us in taking a comprehensive look at the biblical God—the God before whom mountains melt like wax; the God before whom no one yawns. For truly, to catch a genuine glimpse of Yahweh is to clearly understand that humanity has but two options: worship or flee!

As we embark on this sojourn through the Bible together, we joyfully echo the psalmist's exhortation, while we petition God to make it real in each of our lives: "Worship with reverence, rejoice with trembling" (Psalm 2:11). Yes, this is where the born-again lover of Christ must live!

TABLE OF CONTENTS

". . .It is a terrifying thing to fall into the hands of the living God."

Hebrews 10:31

Unpacking the Title

Dangerous God

Wrath, Vengeance, Recompense, and Terror

Dangerous *adj.* 1. Involving or fraught with danger; perilous. 2. Able or apt to do harm.

God *n.* 1. A being conceived as the perfect, omnipotent, omniscient originator and ruler of the universe, the principal object of faith and worship in monotheistic religions.

Wrath *n.* 1. Violent . . . anger; rage; fury. 2. b. Divine retribution for sin.

Vengeance *n.* 1. The act or motive of punishing another in payment for a wrong or injury he has committed; retribution. 2. With great violence or fury.

Recompense *n.* 2. To . . . make return for. Amends made for something, as damage or loss. Payment in return for something given or done. . . .

Terror *n.* 1. Intense, overpowering fear. 2. Something, as a terrifying object or occurrence, that instills intense fear. 3. The ability to instill intense fear.

The perilous and *apt to do harm* . . . *being conceived as the perfect, omnipotent, omniscient originator and ruler of the universe* . . . has promised *violent anger* and *rage* as *divine retribution for sin.* He will *punish* . . . *with great violence* and *fury* . . . *making payment in return for* . . . what man has *done* . . . resulting *in intense, overpowering, terrifying fear.*

*"God has not only told us the best, but He has not withheld
the worst. He has faithfully described the ruin which the Fall
has effected. He has faithfully diagnosed the terrible state
which sin has produced. He has faithfully made known His
enduring hatred of evil, and that He must punish the same.
He has faithfully warned us that He is a "consuming fire."
[And] His Word . . . records numerous examples of His faithfulness in making good His threatenings."*
A.W. Pink
Twentieth-Century Christian Theologian

"God has had it on His heart to show to angels and men not only how excellent His love is, but also how terrible His wrath is."
Jonathan Edwards
Eighteenth-Century Christian Theologian

KEY QUOTES FROM THE INTRODUCTION

God is probably not who you think He is. That is, if you're the average professing Christian, going to your average church.

𝛴

It's time to open the Book and behold the breathtaking awe and terrifying holiness of Jehovah-God.

𝛴

El Shaddai will not countenance being pushed to the periphery of a trivial, religious parody. The biblical God is, by definition, the antithesis of peripheral. He will be central, for He is central whether your preacher and denomination like it or not.

𝛴

It's time to know, believe, and delight in all that God has revealed about Himself. To honestly look at the unredacted God of the Bible is to never be the same.

𝛴

God is unrepentant. He is unapologetic regarding His awful majesty. His anger is splashed all over the pages of Scripture. He has unashamedly revealed exactly who He is for every intelligent being to behold and consider.

☙

If this God, the God of the Bible, is in full view, men and angels have but two viable options— worship or flee! This is what God intends every one of His moral creatures to comprehend in the deepest core of their being.

☙

You, and the God Who Is

1. The opening verse of the book is Hebrews 10:31. What is the clear message of God in Hebrews 10:26–31?

2. What do you learn from the definitions of the words that make up the title and subtitle? Is this the God you worship?

3. What do you take away from the quotes of A. W. Pink and Jonathan Edwards?

4. From the *Prologue*, do you think God is who you
   think He is? How do you know? How can you be
   sure? Why does it matter?

5. The author writes, ". . .El Shaddai will not
   countenance being pushed to the periphery of a
   trivial, religious parody." What is he saying?

6. Do you know and worship the "God of fierce wrath
   and horrifying vengeance?" Do you know and
   worship the God of Nahum 1:2,6?

7. From the *Introduction*, is it possible the church
   has settled for a domesticated, pseudo-christ?
   How important is it for each of us to consider this
   question?

8. What is the author's challenge to the true lover of Christ?

9. What is the author's point regarding the believer's "comprehensive default premise"?

10. What is the genuine disciple's supreme discipline according to Albright? Are you exercising this discipline in your life? How is the psalmist worshiping God in Psalm 94:1–2?

11. What is the author's warning to the nominal churchgoer? Any thoughts?

12. Why do you think the author chose the words he did for the subtitle of the book?

13. Please note your thoughts on the Michael Horton and Tony Reinke quotes. Why should we not apologize for who God says He is?

14. What is the call to both the born-again Christian and the lukewarm one? What insights do you glean from Psalms 2:11, 5:5, 16:4, and 81:15?

15. Do you understand that God is "dreadfully provoked"? Why does this matter to every human being?

KEY QUOTES FROM CHAPTER 1

And with that vision of the "King of glory" on His throne, Isaiah immediately knew two things were inescapably true— God is holy, and he was not.

ᔕ

No more pleasant fictions about who he thought he was before Yahweh. No more divine misconceptions. No more religious delusions. Now, there was no doubt; he was hopelessly exposed.

ᔕ

Tim Challies writes, "The basic human condition is to believe that God isn't really all that holy and that I'm not really that bad. . . . So we are a good match, God and I." This is a miscalculation of infinite and everlasting proportions.

ᔕ

The Scriptures reveal that the supernatural otherness of God evokes an impulsive terror in the heart of humanity.

ℒ

There is nothing more true in all creation than the fact that apart from a saving relationship with Jesus Christ, meeting God will be our greatest trauma! An everlasting and infinite trauma!

ℒ

Every day it is lethal to defy holy God, and His response comes solely at His discretion. It may be immediate as we will see from the pages of Scripture. Or it may come to us at the end of a long, healthy, prosperous, pseudo-Christian life.

ℒ

The world is saturated with obstinate men "given fully" to live unholy lives under the gaze of the Holy. This is idiocy of the highest order.

ℒ

one

3 Times Holy

_____

God's Unapproachable Otherness

1. What is the reason for Isaiah's impassioned lament in Isaiah 6:5? In seeing God, what two things did Isaiah immediately know were true?

2. What do you understand the author to mean in saying that Isaiah was "exhaustively ruined—from the inside out"?

3. How is Isaiah's problem your problem? How do you know you're not holy?

4. What were the reactions of every man in Scripture who was granted a vision of Yahweh? What do you take away from this? Do you agree with the quote from Tim Challies? Please explain why or why not.

5. Any thoughts on Albright's remarks concerning God's holiness and power?

6. Please comment on the author's remarks on God's holiness and magnificence.

7. Any observations on Albright's remarks regarding God's holiness and purity?

8. What is the author's point regarding God's holiness and His otherness?

9. Explain how the holiness of God is the "attribute of attributes".

10. Consider Albright's statement that, "Yes, the biblical God is other. He is the unrivaled Uncreated, the unequaled Unbegun." What are the implications of this statement for every human being?

11. Regarding the lethality of holiness, what do you understand the author to be saying about the possibility of God's judgment coming "to us at the end of a long healthy, prosperous, pseudo-Christian life"?

12. What is your takeaway from the section titled *Holiness and Dereliction*?

13. What do you glean from the section titled *Holiness and Defiance*?

14. What did you learn from the section titled *Holiness and Disobedience*?

15. What lesson did you draw from the section titled *Holiness and Duplicity*?

16. Do you see a connection between Ecclesiastes 8:11 and Romans 2:4–6?

KEY QUOTES FROM CHAPTER 2

One sin brought down paradise. Just one. One sin subjected a two-trillion galaxy cosmos to corruption. I want you to feel the weight and catastrophic scope of that.

ℒ

Make no mistake, every sin is profoundly personal. It's between us and an incensed God—every time.

ℒ

The Scriptures clearly reveal that evil arose from the free will, moral choices of the good but mutable creatures God created.

ℒ

God, while not the author of evil, obviously had good reasons for allowing evil to arise from His good creation—not least being the glory of His Son in the redemption of His people.

ℒ

*Adam's a lot like you and me. He believes he's
a bit of a victim here. Right? I mean, why the
tree? Why the prohibition? Granted there was
only one command but, you know, why the
one? Yeah, and why free will? Couldn't God
have built a more user-friendly cosmos?*

∅

two

1 Sin

God's Just Response

1. Why is the world messed up? What do you learn about God here? What do you learn about man?

2. How is the secular definition of sin inadequate from a biblical perspective? Why is your sin a personal affront to God?

3. What do you think of John Piper's definition of sin? What is the supreme essence of evil? What do you learn from Jeremiah 2:11–13?

4. How good did Adam and Eve have it in the Garden? How did God stack the deck in their favor regarding their moral obligation toward Him?

5. What do you learn about Satan from Ezekiel 28:16,17 and Isaiah 14:13–14?

6. If God is both good and omnipotent, why does evil exist? Was evil a created thing? How are the analogies of darkness and cold helpful here?

7. Albright writes, "Obviously, to say evil came *from* God is blasphemous. But to in turn say, evil did not come *by* God is equally blasphemous. Evil has come *by* good but not *from* good." What do you understand him to be saying?

8. What is Satan attacking in his exchange with Eve? How was she equipped to deal with this challenge? What are Satan's favorite lies?

9. How do you understand C. S. Lewis' point about Adam and Eve wanting to be nouns but that they could only ever be adjectives?

10. How did Adam and Eve find God after they sinned? Who was seeking whom? What do we learn about ourselves from Romans 3:10–18, Jeremiah 17:9, Ecclesiastes 9:3, 1 Corinthians 2:14, and Romans 8:7?

11. Albright writes, "It's why pseudo-churches are full of people—all hiding from God in the most inconspicuous place." What is the author saying?

12. What is the most beautiful question in human history? What if that question had never been asked? What is the origin of human victimhood? Why is it dangerous?

13. What do you take away from John Piper's quote regarding calamity and suffering in the world?

14. In light of the fact that one sin brought down the whole cosmos, what is the inevitable question that emerges in the thinking person's mind?

KEY QUOTES FROM CHAPTER 3

God created man to live. We knowingly chose
death. We did that. And death is coming for
each of us. . .very, very soon.

ॐ

Yes, God is love but obviously, as God, His
emotional life is infinitely complex. He is more
than one thing. Just as you and I are. "God is
love" but He is also "fierce wrath."

ॐ

We're either Bible believers or we're not. The
true Christian doesn't stand in judgment over
God's Word. We don't presume to have the
right to pick and choose what to believe and
what to mythologize.

ॐ

God does not put the life of man above His
glory. When once His longsuffering patience
has been exhausted, He will be glorified in
executing perfect justice.

ॐ

We must always remember: God is under no obligation to save anyone. He is the Potter; He can do whatever He wants with "the thing molded."

♨

The judgments of the Flood, and Sodom and Gomorrah, are but a modest salvo in God's shock-and-awe assault on those who are in conscious rebellion against Him.

♨

three

2 RIGHTEOUS VERDICTS

God Rains Down Justice

1. Albright writes, "False teachers tell us that God will not judge humanity because He is constrained by His love. Well, the false teachers are refuted 150,000 plus times per day." What is his point here?

2. How do you understand Albright's assertion "that all of God does all that God does?" How does John Piper's quote help in this regard?

3. Many today mock the account of Noah, the ark, the animals, and the flood. What did Jesus Christ say (Matthew 24:37–39)? What do you say? So. . .why the flood?

4. A Challenge Question: Why do you think many who profess to be Christians mythologize the first eleven chapters of Genesis? Why is this a fatal error?

5. How many died in the flood? Albright writes, "This is God's prerogative. There is an important lesson here for us. God does not put the life of man above His glory." What is the author saying?

6. Is God under any obligation to save anyone? Albright writes, "God never offered the [fallen] angels a savior. He simply gave them what their rebellion warranted—justice." Any thoughts?

7. Why is Abraham's question about sweeping away
    the righteous with the wicked noteworthy? Are you,
    like Abraham, doing the cultural math? What do
    you deduce from this exercise regarding our culture
    today?

8. What do we learn about Sodom from Genesis
    19:4–5, 24–25, 28? Only four were saved from the
    conflagration. Any thoughts?

9. What do you learn from Jesus' words about Lot's
    wife (Luke 17:32–33)? What do you take away from
    Eugene Peterson's paraphrases of the Lord's words?

10. In our contemporary culture, what does compassion
    demand in speaking God's truth about all sexual
    sin, including homosexuality?

11. Some say Jesus never said homosexuality was sin.
    Why is this obviously false? Some say those who
    call homosexuality sin are engaging in hate-speech.
    How is this obviously false?

12. What do we learn about freedom from all sin in
    1 Corinthians 6:9–11?

13. What is God's clear warning in Isaiah 5:20–21 and
    Romans 1:32?

KEY QUOTES FROM CHAPTER 4

Moses faced the same decision each one of us faces. To align ourselves with the wealth, power, prestige, comfort, security, pleasure, and luxury of this world, or to align ourselves with God and His invincible purposes.
Each of us must weigh it out.

ℒ

It is a God-ordained verity, you will eternally reap whatever you temporally sow.

ℒ

Pharaoh is resting comfortably in his luxurious palace completely unaware that he has already been irrevocably judged by his Creator.
Nothing has changed outwardly,
but it is all over inwardly.

ℒ

Only narcissistic fools play games with Jehovah.

ℒ

God was relentless in His wrath poured out
upon Egypt as He will be against every person
who chooses to remain His adversary.
In effect, God says this is personal.
Sin always is with God.

ℒ

The Egyptian king will ultimately have no
choice but to acknowledge that Yahweh is God.
Truly, it will be the ever-present realization
that will utterly overwhelm and grip his
mind for a billion eternities in hell.

ℒ

four

O First Born Spared

God in Their Midst

1. Albright opens the chapter with the statement "God in Their Midst." It comes from Exodus 11:4–5 regarding the death plague. The opening verse in the chapter is Amos 9:4. What do you learn about God from these texts?

2. Moses, like all of us, had to weigh out the sowing and reaping principle. What do you learn about his choice from Hebrews 11:24–26? What have you chosen?

3. In having a supernatural encounter with Creator-God, Moses tries to excuse himself multiple times from

God's call. Why? What mistake is Moses making?

4. What do you learn about God's ways in judgment
   in how He judged Pharaoh? Is it right for God
   to harden a man's heart, to give him over to
   damnation? Why?

5. What was God's ultimate purpose in raising up
   Pharoah?

6. A Challenge Question: Theodicy is the vindication
   of divine goodness in view of the existence of evil
   in the world. How is Romans 9:22–23 the ultimate
   theodicy?

7. What is the one thing the saved and the damned
   forever have in common?

8. According to Albright, what do we learn about God in the account of the ten plagues?

9. What does Albright say we learn about man in the account of the ten plagues?

10. What other lessons do you draw in reviewing the ten plagues?

11. What do we learn about feigned repentance from the plague accounts?

12. What lessons do you draw from Exodus 11:4–5, 9, 12:12? How is sin a personal affront to God?

13. A Challenge Question: How is it a divine right to give or take life?

14. How does the Exodus Passover point to Jesus Christ?

15. What does Albright mean when he says, "It's not that men don't know, it's that they do"?

16. How did Israel respond to God's destruction of Pharaoh's army at the Red Sea?

17. What does Albright mean in asserting that "There will be no unbelievers in hell"?

Key Quotes from Chapter 5

Jehovah is awesome. He is fearsome. He is dreadful. He is frightening. This is all true because He is holy-other. He provokes fear, trembling, and terror in the heart of fallen man.

☙

Sometimes God is longsuffering. Sometimes He is not. Premeditated, habitual, lifestyle sin against God, garnished with a little pseudo-Christianity, is like a perpetual game of Russian Roulette. Sooner or later, with sudden finality, you die—forever.

☙

The genuine Christian is always willing to tremble before God, but never, never, never call Him to account for His actions.

☙

Remember that whenever you find yourself recoiling at God's ways in judgment, you must never forget two simple things. He is always right. And you are always wrong.

ℒ

It's one of the indisputable lessons of the Bible—when once God is aroused to destruction, He is proficient.

ℒ

Lest you bow to the terrifyingly magnificent God of the Bible, the One who kills men, women, boys, and girls in accordance with His righteous judgments—wrath, vengeance, recompense, and terror will soon be yours.

ℒ

five

33 KINGDOMS ANNIHILATED

God's Instrument of Wrath

1. From Genesis 15:12, why would there be "terror and great darkness" as God met with Abraham?

2. What do you learn about God from the Exodus and Hebrews passages cited in the Chapter introduction? (See footnotes 3 and 4 in the book for this.) Is the God you worship like this?

3. What do we learn about God's ways in judgment from Genesis 15:16?

4. Albright says the Amorites are in the midst of a Romans Chapter 1 judgment (see Romans 1:18–32). What do you understand this to mean?

5. The inhabitants of Canaan were not cognizant of the fact they had already been irrevocably judged. What do you take away from this biblical reality?

6. From Deuteronomy 4:33–35, what was the takeaway for the Exodus Jews in seeing God's mighty judgment against Egypt?

7. What does God mean for men to know and understand when He unleashes judgment?

8. From Deuteronomy 7:2, 7:10, what was God's instruction to the Exodus Jews regarding the peoples of Canaan?

9. From Leviticus 26:1–12 and 14–30, what was God's promise and warning to the Hebrews? Why would any thinking person decide against this God?

10. In Exodus 32 and Numbers 25:3–4, we see the rebellion of the people against God. How is this possible after all they had witnessed? What is God's response?

11. What is Albright's response to those who are offended at the command of God's prophet, Moses, to kill all the boys and every woman who had known a man intimately but to save the virgin girls (Numbers 31:14–15, 17–18)? What does the true believer never do?

12. What lessons do you draw from Albright's summary of God's utter annihilation of the kingdoms of Canaan? How do you respond to those who denounce God for this?

13. From Joshua 21:43–45 and 24:19–20, what do we see regarding God's faithfulness in blessing and His faithfulness in judgment?

14. What is Albright's warning as he closes the chapter? What are your thoughts?

KEY QUOTES FROM CHAPTER 6

God hates mere religion. He always has. Jesus Christ didn't mince His words. He pronounced damnation upon the religious leaders of His day.

⌘

Religion is Satan's best con. He's the "father of lies." And his religious fictions are taking billions to hell. It's the ultimate demonic scam.

⌘

Denominational banality and rote ecclesiastical performance are simply a lot less bothersome than true repentance and unconditional obedience—the explicit call of the Son of God to anyone who would claim Him as Lord and Savior.

⌘

A lot of people like church just fine as long as an emasculated god is served up.

⌘

God is not unclear about mere religious
performance—He loathes it!

⌇

In thoughtfully considering the awful vengeance
of God in the physical realm, you will in turn get
some small sense of how monstrous your sin
is in the spiritual realm.

⌇

Thankfully, Yahweh is a full-disclosure God.
We're not left to grope for truth in a vacuum.
He has spoken. The Bible is clear. He is a
magnificent Savior and yes,
He is a fearsome Judge.

⌇

six

12 Prophets Proclaim Fury

God's Promised Consequence

1. Albright closes Chapter 5 with Jeremiah 4:18 and
    begins Chapter 6 with Ezekiel 7:3, 7. What critical
    truth do we draw from these texts regarding God's
    judgment?

2. What do you draw from the author's discussion on
    "religion" as opposed to genuine Christianity? Why
    is religion easier than born-again Christianity?

3. What are the shocking things the Old Testament
    Jews said to the prophets (Isaiah 30:9–10)?

4. What are the shocking things the apostle Paul says professing Christians will desire during this age (2 Timothy 4:3-4)?

5. From verses listed under footnote 6, how do Jeremiah's words to apostate Judah apply to modern, apostate Christianity?

6. What does Albright say God loathes and crushes? What does Psalm 81:15 reveal?

7. What is the author's challenge in reading the words of the Old Testament prophets? He writes, "God might very well use His words on the next few pages to dramatically alter the rest of your life. . .and beyond!" Is it an overstatement?

8. What is God saying through Obadiah, "As you have done, it will be done to you. Your dealings will return on your head"?

9. God says through Hosea that "Their deeds will not allow them to return to their God" and that "the LORD has withdrawn from them." What is the prophet saying?

10. A Challenge Question: Hosea writes that "their little ones will be dashed to pieces and their pregnant women will be ripped open." Why does this kind of evil exist and why is man wholly responsible? (Review *The Inevitable Question* section in Chapter Two and revisit the first question of that lesson.)

11. Note at least one thing that stood out to you from the summary of each of the following books— Amos, Micah, Zephaniah, Nahum, Habakkuk, Zechariah.

12. Note at least one thing that impacted you from the summary of Isaiah, Ezekiel, Jeremiah, and Lamentations.

13. What does the author mean that God is "a full-disclosure God"?

14. What does Albright mean that God is both pure delight and comprehensive horror?

KEY QUOTES FROM CHAPTER 7

God's fierce adjudications upon the earth
are only the beginning of an unending,
omnipotent cascade of divine fury. More wrath
is coming. Infinitely more. Everlastingly more.

⌖

We're all living on the edge of eternity. Forever
is but one heartbeat away. Understanding
Messiah's teaching here matters far more than
anything else you've got going on right now.

⌖

The Bible reveals, however, that the horror of
temporal judgment is but a faint glimmer of that
which is to come—namely, divine
indignation beyond the grave.

⌖

Infinite outrage awaits every unrepentant soul.
Provoked holiness knows no bounds.

⌖

What's at stake in a deep understanding of the doctrine of hell? Nothing less than a right comprehension of your God, your worship, your sin, and His cross.

✍

Without question, eternal, conscious punishment is the most hated doctrine in the Bible, but it is the indisputably clear teaching of God incarnate. Hell is real. It is forever. Jesus Christ said so.

✍

In a very broad stroke summary, Jesus Christ said hell is real. He said it is eternal. It is terrible. It is deserved. And once there, it is inescapable.

✍

seven

9 TEACHINGS OF JESUS CHRIST

God's Eternal Sentence

1. How do the words of Jesus Christ regarding judgment enlarge and intensify what we have already seen in our study thus far? Why must we, as Albright writes, "allow our mind's eye to adjust to a kind of timeless farsightedness"?

2. Contemplate the definition of *eternal*. Look at every synonym. Then read and comment on Jonathan Edward's quote regarding eternal, conscious punishment.

3. Why does Albright contend that wrath, vengeance, recompense, and terror forever are an indispensable doctrine? Why does it matter every day?

4. Who was the most outspoken hell-fire preacher in the New Testament? What were His teachings on hell?

5. How does Albright indict much of the modern church regarding the biblical doctrine of hell? How does he bring "intellectual integrity" into the discussion?

6. What phrase does Jesus use most often in describing hell? Why is there weeping? Why is there gnashing of teeth?

7. How is the baseline truth of humanity revealed in hell? What is C. S. Lewis' point regarding the "doors of hell being locked on the inside"?

8. Did you know that God was in hell? What did you learn from that section?

9. Review all the Scripture noted supporting the doctrine of eternal, conscious punishment for those who remain in rebellion against God. Would your average eight-year-old be convinced?

10. What do you take away from the chapter section "You Thought I Was Just Like You"?

11. What are the two principal reasons given to rebut the argument that temporal sin could not warrant eternal punishment? Are you convinced? Why?

12. What are the most prominent false teachings against eternal damnation? What is the most glaring fault in these arguments?

13. Any thoughts on the section "The Mirror, or God"?

14. According to Albright, what is the paramount lesson from the Luke 16 parable? What did you think of the A. W. Pink quote he used to close the chapter?

KEY QUOTES FROM CHAPTER 8

Dread and horror fill the pages of God's final book. It's Yahweh's promise to all who have willfully made themselves His enemy.

❧

No impenitent person will stand in the face of God's omnipotent fury. Indeed, as the apostle writes, they will prefer suicide to standing before the angry Lamb.

❧

Lamb-phobia is no exaggerated dread. The angry Lamb is the consummate human horror! And there will never be any escape from His terrifying presence—forever!

❧

So, what are the holiest of saints in heaven praying about? Your average church member would never guess. I mean, they would never, ever guess. John tells us these holy ones are praying for one thing—vengeance!

❧

It's the sub-biblical, post-Christian, contemporary view of God which portrays Him as merely love; only love. . .nothing but love.

ℒ

No true believer pretends to be more longsuffering and compassionate than God. We, like our Father, have a taste for this—for the glory of God in His spent wrath.

ℒ

All pseudo Christs will be conspicuously absent on the last day. Only the angry Lamb will be in view. Every eye will be on Him as He meticulously and fiercely answers the heavenly prayer for vengeance.

ℒ

The 66th book is unambiguous. Jesus Christ is coming. Judgment is coming. Wrath is coming. Vengeance is coming. The second death is coming. This will happen.
You will see it.

ℒ

eight

66ᵀᴴ Book

God's End-Times Judgment

1. Albright opens the chapter by saying that "Lamb-phobia is no exaggerated dread. The angry Lamb is the consummate human horror!" What is he saying?

2. Early in the chapter, Albright revisits his subtitle. Any thoughts on these biblical words after working through the first seven chapters of the book?

3. The author states that "God is invincibly faithful. He always delivers on a promise." What point is he making here?

4. For what are the saints in heaven praying? Any thoughts? How did Jesus talk about it in Luke 18:6–8? According to Albright, who understands and loves this prayer?

5. Albright writes, "We, like our Father, have a taste. . .for the glory of God in His spent wrath." What are the multitudes in heaven singing? Why? What are your thoughts?

6. What does Romans 12:19–21 tell us about vengeance? What is the command of 1 Peter 3:8–9? Will you obey the Lord in this?

7. What counsel does the author offer those who dare to disregard Revelation? What do you take away from Revelation 1:13–16, 5:8–13, and 22:18–19?

8. According to 1 Peter 4:17–18, where does judgment begin? How do we see this in Revelation?

9. What do we learn about the churches of Ephesus, Pergamum, Thyatira, Sardis, and Laodicea? What was the sin of each? How do we see this in the contemporary church?

10. Any thoughts on the author's comments under the chapter section "God Gags"?

11. Francis Chan writes, "Something is wrong when our lives make sense to unbelievers." What do you think? Is he right? Why or why not?

12. How did Jesus talk about false Christians in the church? (See Matthew 13:30, 41–42.)

13. What is your takeaway regarding the fierce wrath of God as recorded in the book of Revelation?

14. What is the compelling message of God's 66th book?

KEY QUOTES FROM CHAPTER 9

Scripture is alarmingly blunt: left to our own devices, we would all land in hell. This is who we are. We are utterly damned without His overture.

☙

I-AM-El-Shaddai God is in a manger! Let the whole created order and every thinking, sentient being in it, stand in stunned, staggered, breathless awe!

☙

If you think God took on flesh and was crucified principally because of you, you've been utterly misinformed.

☙

Was the coming and crucifixion of the Son an ad hoc, stop-gap, eleventh-hour remedy for an unforeseen decision of man? No! It was a done deal on the far side of eternity past!

☙

Who was in on the murder of Jesus Christ? Yes, the Jews. Yes, the Gentiles. But principally, this was the plan of Triune God. What men of their own free will meant for evil— God meant for good.

God has come to be butchered for His bride. This is God's remedy to the looming wrath, vengeance, recompense, and terror problem all the sons and daughters of Adam have before their Creator.

ℒ

The Son has come for the Triune God's glory and for the joy of His ransomed people. Breathtaking!

ℒ

To really believe is to be utterly changed from the inside out. As every born-again Christian can testify, it is the only life worth living.

ℒ

So, do you really believe? The test is never in merely believing the facts. The test is always in loving the Christ—delighting in Him and building your "walking around life" upon Him.

ℒ

nine

6 HOURS

God's Remedy

1. What is the root issue and bottom-line question Albright is asking the reader in the first few paragraphs?

2. What is the shocking reality we learn about ourselves in Romans 3:10–12?

3. God in a manger! How do the quotes from Charles Spurgeon and J. I. Packer challenge you in thinking about the incarnation of the Son?

4. What is Albright's assertion regarding God's ultimate reason and purpose in saving sinners? Why is this important?

5. What do you learn from the Joe Rigney quote?

6. Why does the author find it difficult to preach on Christmas and Easter?

7. How does Albright link Ephesians 2:1–3 and the Christmas account?

8. Was God caught unawares when man sinned? When did God save His people? Whose idea was the crucifixion?

9. Why is "why?" the wrong question? What is the right question?

10. What do you understand Albright to be saying about the "Muzak" Christian?

11. Who is this riding into Jerusalem on a donkey? Think deeply about this. Any thoughts?

12. What do we learn *about* Jesus from the Gospel accounts regarding His arrest?

13. What do you glean from Albright's comments concerning the scourging of God?

14. What does the author say is a good "why?" question? Do you agree? Why?

15. Why does Mary Magdalene believe? Why do you believe?

16. What does Jesus mean when He says, "You do not believe because you are not My sheep"?

17. What does John say about how we can know we belong to God?

KEY QUOTES FROM THE EPILOGUE

The bottom-line truth here is that both God's detractors and His lukewarm followers find Him and His wisdom tedious, irrelevant, yes. . .foolish. *Fool* is the epithet of all in hell.

ℐ

. . .Isaiah 66:2 raises the urgent and unavoidably obvious questions—Are you in fact humble and contrite before Him? Are you willing, yes eager, to tremble at His Word?

ℐ

The Isaiah 66:2 injunctions are not a rational or logical challenge for us—in fact, they are intuitively necessary for anyone paying much attention at all.

ℐ

To tremble before God and His Word is no real stretch for the average IQ!

ℐ

. . .you can fear your Creator the easy way—in humility, contrition, and reverence or, you can fear Him the hard way—as the end result of a self-glorifying, God-ignoring life.

✍

Concerning your average biblical skeptic, may I share that I've never personally encountered one who had actually put any effort into his conviction.

✍

No, you don't get to play the middle with the Bible. You're either all in, or you're not in at all.

✍

Where are you standing? On rock, or sand? Are you a wise man or a fool? It is not only evident today—it will be evident every single moment of forever.

✍

epilogue

You, and the Word God Has Given

---

1. What do you learn about the fool from Psalm 53:1, Proverbs 12:15, 1 Corinthians 2:14, 1:18?

2. Albright states, "There is no ultimate distinction between the militant unbeliever and the nominal believer." What do you understand him to be saying?

3. What is the beginning of wisdom? How does the wise man apply Isaiah 66:2? How are you obeying Isaiah 66:2?

4. Why are the Isaiah 66:2 injunctions not a rational or logical challenge for the true believer?

5. Based upon Albright's arguments, why do you think he writes the following sentence? "To tremble before God and His Word is no stretch for the average IQ!"

6. The author states that all will fear God, one way or the other. What is his point?

7. Albright states, ". . .once you discount the Bible, all you have left at best is human speculation, or worse, demonic deception." Do you agree or disagree? Why?

8. What claim does the Bible make?

9. What does God say about His Word from the following passages? Isaiah 40:8, Isaiah 55:11, Deuteronomy 8:3, Matthew 5:18, John 10:35, 2 Timothy 3:16, 2 Peter 1:20–21.

10. How is the Bible utterly unique?

11. How are attacks on the Bible actually attacks on God?

12. What are the varied evidences that the Bible is the Word of God? How does John Piper talk about the paramount assurance the believer has regarding the Bible?

13. Regarding eternity—why is "the ball squarely in your court"?

14. What is your view of the Bible? Are you standing on rock or sand? (See Matthew 7:24–27.)

15. From Isaiah 65:1, Deuteronomy 30:19, Ezekiel 33:11 (NKJV), what is God's statement and invitation?

16. What does the writer of Hebrews tell us in Hebrews 10:26–27?

KEY QUOTES FROM APPENDICES 1 & 2

For indeed, to genuinely fear the biblical God
is to fear nothing else. To fear the biblical God
is to be progressively liberated from every form
of anxiety and temporal slavery.

ℒ

The proper fear of God—this stunned wonder
and captivated reverence—fully animates
the human spirit and intellect. To walk in
perpetual amazement of Yahweh
is to be truly alive!

ℒ

We cannot settle for merely attending religious
services and knowing biblical facts. We must
encounter and know our Creator-Redeemer
God in all His fullness.

ℒ

For in rightly looking at the biblical God, we
can no longer see ourselves as victims but as
the rebels we've always been.

ℒ

And how does the born-again person mature
in the fear of God? It's simple. Look at Him.
You must relentlessly look at God in
His Word to grow the fear.

ℒ

In the seeking of God, and in the looking at
God, we are, for the first time in our lives,
learning real freedom.

ℒ

You must decide. Will you practice the fear of
God? Meaning, will you live it out? Will you do
it every day?

ℒ

Fearing our Creator is life. It is purpose. It is
meaning. It is fulfillment. It is joy.

ℒ

appendices
1 & 2

FEARING GOD

---

1. What is the simple but life-and-eternity-impacting truth of Ecclesiastes 8:12?

2. Albright opens with this sentence: "The fear of God is the most beautiful, powerful, meaningful, fulfilling, and yes, exuberant place to live. If you call yourself a Christian and don't know that—you're doing it wrong." What do you think about this assertion?

3. Albright asserts that "to fear God is to fear nothing else." Do you agree? Why?

4. For you, what are the most interesting comments the author makes in the first five paragraphs of Appendix 1?

5. What did you think of the author's summary of how "belief unfolded for some readers"?

6. What is the biblical prescription for finding the fear of the Lord? What is God's promise in this regard?

7. How does looking at God in the Word help us to understand that we are not victims and that, indeed, "everything is grace"?

8. What do you take away from the section entitled *Growing Fear—It's in the Looking*?

9. Any insights from the section entitled *Living Fear—It's in the Emancipation*?

10. What do you learn from the section *Practicing Fear—It's in the Obedience*?

11. Any comments on the section, *Unpacking Fear—It's in the Delight*? What do you learn from the following verses? Nehemiah 1:11 (ESV), Psalm 2:11, Isaiah 11:2-3.

12. How do you understand the following quote from John Piper? "There is a terror when outside of Christ and a different kind of trembling when in Christ."

13. What is the thrill of fear? What is Piper's point here?

14. What are God's promises to those who fear the Lord?

15. How does Albright answer the *Fair Question*? What is his point regarding the *Plausible Inference*?

KEY QUOTES FROM APPENDIX 3

"If God should forever cast you off, it would
be exactly agreeable to your treatment of
Him. . .you, who never have exercised the least
degree of love to God in all your life. . . ."

&

"You care not what becomes of God's glory;
you are not distressed how much His honor
seems to suffer in the world: why should God
care anymore for your welfare?"

&

"Are you more honorable than God, that He
must be obliged to make much of you, how
light however you make of Him
and His glory?"

&

"As God has multiplied mercies, so you have
multiplied provocations."

&

"Consider how often you have refused to hear God's calls to you, and how just it would therefore be, if He should refuse to hear you when you call to Him."

ℒ

"Do you think. . .that you may be an enemy to God, but God must by no means be an enemy to you. . . ?"

ℒ

appendix 3

THE JUSTICE OF GOD IN THE DAMNATION
OF SINNERS

Share your thoughts on the following quotes from Jonathan Edwards' famous sermon addressed to the impenitent, including those who are nominal Christians.

1. "[God] is originally under no obligation to keep men from sinning; but may in His providence permit and leave them to sin. . .It is unreasonable to suppose, that God should be obliged, if He makes a reasonable creature capable of knowing His will, and receiving a law from Him, and being subject to His moral government, at the same time to make it impossible for [angels or men] to sin or break His law. . . ."

2. ". . .God by His sovereignty has a right to determine about [man's] redemption as He pleases. He has a right to determine whether He will redeem any or not. He might, if He had pleased, have left all to perish. . . ."

3. "You have voluntarily chosen to be with Satan in his
    enmity and opposition to God; how justly therefore
    might you be with him in his punishment! You have
    given yourself up to [Satan]. . .how justly therefore
    may God also give you up to him, and leave you in
    his power, to accomplish your ruin!"

4. "Have you not taken encouragement to sin against
    God, on that very presumption, that God would show
    you mercy when you sought it? And may not God
    justly refuse you that mercy upon which you have so
    presumed? . . . how righteous therefore would it be
    in God, to disappoint such a wicked presumption! It
    was upon that very hope that you dared to affront the
    majesty of heaven so dreadfully as you have done; and
    can you now be so [foolish] as to think that God is
    obliged not to frustrate that hope?"

5. "You have taken encouragement to sin the more,
    for [the] consideration that Christ came in the
    world and died to save sinners; You would take the
    pleasures of sin still longer, hardening yourself
    because mercy was infinite, and it would not be too
    late, if you sought it afterwards; now, how justly
    may God disappoint you in this, and so order it that
    it shall be too late!"

6. "The heinousness of this sin of rejecting a Savior especially appears in two things: (1) The greatness of the benefits offered. (2) The wonderfulness of the way in which these benefits are procured and offered. . .Herein you have exceeded the devils; for they never rejected the offers of such glorious mercy; no, nor any mercy at all. This will be the distinguishing condemnation of gospel-sinners. . . ."

7. You would have your own way, and did not like that God should oppose you in it, and your way was to ruin your own soul; how just therefore is it, if now at length, God ceases to oppose you, and falls in with you, and lets your soul be ruined; and as you would destroy yourself, so should put to His hand to destroy you too!"

ABOUT THE AUTHOR

At the age of forty-two, Jim left a twenty-year business career to answer God's call to preach. Since early 2004, he and his wife, Karen, have lived in Milan, Italy, where Jim is the pastor of the International Church of Milan, a non-denominational, Bible-believing, and Bible-teaching church ministering to internationals from every corner of the globe. He is also author of *Uncareful Lives: Walking Where Feet May Fail* (Ambassador Publications) and *Everything Says, "Glory!": Science Exposes Darwinian Folklore* (Great Writing Publications).

Learn more about Jim Albright at
http://www.greatwriting.org/author-albright

You can find Jim's sermons at
https://pastorjimpodcast.podbean.com/

www.dangerousgod.com

Dangerous God
Wrath, Vengeance, Recompense, and Terror
Jim Albright
Trade Paperback, 8.5 x 5.5 inches, 176pp

ISBN: 978-1-7343452-4-7

CPSIA information can be obtained
at www.ICGtesting.com
Printed in the USA
LVHW010150170322
713569LV00014B/1884

9 781735 949192